DAVID CURRELL

D1545502

Puppetry for School Children

CHARLES T. BRANFORD COMPANY
NEWTON, MASSACHUSETTS 02159

Phototypeset by BAS Printers Limited, Wallop, Hampshire
Printed in Great Britain by
Fletcher & Son Ltd, Norwich, Norfolk
and bound by
Richard Clay (The Chaucer Press) Ltd, Bungay, Suffolk
for the Publishers
Charles T. Branford Company
28 Union Street, Newton Centre
Massachusetts 02159

CONTENTS

F.E.L.R.P.

To Gordon Staight,
a puppet master who taught me
all I know about puppets

1   Claire and Katie with their 'sock' puppets

FOREWORD

Puppetry has been developing as a valuable creative form of expression in schools for a number of years. It has long been regarded as an art form which unites creative English on the one hand with visual art on the other.

Through the medium of puppetry children are enabled to develop their imaginations to the full. A child's love of fantasy can be given full play and the basic need to act out situations is completely fulfilled, even for withdrawn personalities who find the indirect expression of puppetry so much easier than alternative means of self-expression such as play-acting. Through puppetry, the opportunity exists for expression through mime and movement, speech, creative writing, costume and scenic design, lighting, and, of course, through modelling and construction work in the making of the puppet.

Few would disagree that an ideal opportunity exists for the fusion of art forms while the child is in the primary school. At this time learning is largely under the direction and guidance of one teacher so there is the opportunity for complete integration of study to take place, and puppetry is an ideal catalyst through which much of this integration may be possible.

Many primary school teachers have approached the idea of using puppetry rather tentatively or have shown luke-warm interest only, because it is commonly felt that the subject cannot be developed very fully with children up to the age of eleven, and that a 'dead end' is reached after a few elementary exercises. The subject is often regarded as being too difficult technically—beyond the capabilities of the children and outside the experience of the teacher.

The great value of this book lies in the fact that the author has set out deliberately to show how effectively puppetry can be incorporated into the life of the primary school child. Stage by stage he outlines the possibilities of the subject and illustrates how simply it can be introduced as an effective art form with young children.

David Currell is not only an expert puppeteer but has gained valuable and wide experience of teaching primary school children with whom his exciting and stimulating methods have achieved great success.

Already, leading educationalists have pin-pointed the great value of puppetry in a teaching situation. David Currell brings his own expertise as a puppeteer to the teaching situation and demonstrates in a practical manner what any enthusiastic primary school teacher might achieve with minimal equipment and only a slight prior knowledge of the subject.

R. E. SLATER, NDD, ATD
Principal Lecturer in Art and
Head of the Art Department,
College of St Mark and St John, Chelsea

Part One
PUPPETRY IN THE PRIMARY SCHOOL

WHY DO PUPPETRY?

Children, in their play, animate a great variety of objects and to some extent may be recognised as 'puppeteers'. Puppetry is an art, but the teacher may also find it to be an excellent way of integrating the subjects in the school curriculum and of breaking down the very artificial barriers that have been set up.

History, geography, art, craft, science, and French, as well as English, may all be encompassed by this medium. It would, of course, be unwise for a teacher to try to manipulate a subject to fit in if it does not do so naturally. Such artificial links may well break down themselves.

If used in the right way, puppetry can become a dynamic medium in the field of education, and if the teacher has a deeper knowledge of this art, of its possibilities, limitations, and techniques, he will be better equipped to maximise its potential. In the journals of the Puppeteers of America may be found a detailed description of an experiment carried out by the New York Board of Education to determine 'the effectiveness of using puppetry in the school to enrich and aid the language arts programme'. Classes from the kindergarten right through to the 8th grade participated, using shadow puppets, glove puppets, marionettes and masks.

It was found that, through puppetry, the children became aware of the importance of sequence in story-telling, they enriched their vocabularies, held discussions on the plot, script, and production, and took an interest in classical music in order to find appropriate music for their plays. They also had to carry out research into the topic, and this included work in the areas of geography, history, and current affairs. There was evident eagerness to improve speech, and the problem children, finding that they were depended upon to do their share, did a good job.

This, however, is only a part of what can be achieved through puppetry. Topics in school expand and lead off into many varied avenues of exploration; so it is with puppetry. In this book I have attempted to show how the art of puppetry may be employed to great advantage educationally, but the ideas contained herein are intended only as suggestions. They are approaches which I have tried and have found to be successful for me and for the children I have taught; others may have a greater degree of success with an alternative method or with a development of my suggestions. There are no hard and fast rules; the only test that need be applied is: Does it work? If it works, use it. It is part of the fun of puppetry to try new ideas and develop old ones.

2   Joseph is warned of Herod's evil plan
Pleasure and concentration, clearly evident here, are so often present with puppetry

PUPPETRY IN THE NURSERY
AND INFANT SCHOOL

In these sections of the primary school will be felt the effect
of puppetry in terms of socialisation and integration,
perhaps more than in any other part of the education
system. The children will naturally be very demanding of
the teacher so it may be found advisable to begin with only
one group, so that if others join in gradually, those with
experience would then be able to offer assistance to their
peers.

If the children should wish to be hidden, a simple theatre
may be erected in seconds by draping an old clothes-horse
with a sheet or simply by performing from below table-level.
With regard to the form the puppet 'plays' will take, these
children will often choose to *ad lib*, drawing upon their
common experiences, either in school or at home, for their
subject-matter. Also popular are dramatisations of familiar
folk stories or nursery rhymes.

In addition to having a variety of materials at hand for
puppet-making, it is also wise to have available a selection
of stock characters that might be met in everyday life, such
as the mother, the father, the teacher, the doctor, and so on.
Times will arise when the children have an idea that they
want to implement at once, and delay will cause
disappointment and frustration to such young children if
they have to wait until they have made a new set of puppets,
so they could turn to the standard stock to satisfy their
immediate needs.

I have great reservations about whether a puppet show
presented by a puppeteer is really suitable for nursery
school children whatever the content of the show. Of its
suitability for infants I have no doubt, provided that the
material is carefully selected, but my own experience and
further enquiries have led me to believe that nursery school

3   Busy hands of six-year-olds at work on glove puppets

children are generally far happier with little plays
presented by their companions.

PUPPETRY IN THE JUNIOR SCHOOL

By the time they reach the junior school, the children will often be beginning to develop a desire for plot and suspense. They frequently have ideas, especially weird and wonderful effects, which they are unable to carry out without help. In such a situation the teacher should remain a guide, retaining a democratic role and not falling into the trap of swamping the young puppeteers with his own ideas.

Puppets are often a great help to shy children who lose a lot of their inhibitions and fears when hidden by the puppet theatre and speaking through a puppet. They are a great stimulus to the imagination, often much greater than the stimulus of a picture. Also, if the children are to adapt a simple story into a puppet play, they will have to be selective in choosing the important points which must be brought out; they will, in fact, be approaching a simple form of précis. Other points that children may be brought to understand are dealt with in the section on writing the script.

It is possible to present an anthology of poetry with puppets: each child delivers a piece in keeping with the character of the puppet he is manipulating, and the children really do try to speak in character rather than fall into the 'sing-song' which is all too common. I have found that children will put far more feeling and expression into what they say when it is tackled via the medium of puppetry.

One possible approach to obtain a play intended to be produced for an audience is as follows:

1   The story is chosen, either from a book, from history, or written by a child
2   The children discuss how to split it up into scenes, and what needs to be revealed in each scene
3   The class divides into groups. Each group takes a scene

and prepares the script, either by impromptu acting or by discussion
4   The scenes are put together and any discrepancies between them are corrected

Alternatively, the teacher may decide to tackle it thus:

1   The story is chosen
2   It is split up into scenes through group or class discussion
3   The children take parts and act it impromptu all the way through whilst a tape recording is made

If the standard of the recording is not very high (because of the difficulties involved in taping an impromptu play), the script may be re-recorded under more favourable conditions now that its contents are known. This recording is used when the play is presented, and the puppets will act to it.

After the first recording has been made, the teacher may feel that he wishes to transcribe this and have a written script. There are hazards involved in using a recording for a performance, the greatest danger being the possibility of a hitch in the action (such as a misplaced puppet off-stage) whilst the tape-recorded script runs on; the alternative of stopping the tape is the only action possible but this leaves a long, clumsy break in the scene. If the parts are being spoken 'live' during the performance, any hitches can be smoothed over by a few extra sentences spoken impromptu by the speakers if they have been prepared for such an occasion.

The teacher must decide whether he is prepared to risk having a hitch and thus have all the children free to be stage-hands and manipulators, whether he wishes to have the manipulators learn and speak their own parts, or whether he wishes to have half the children manipulating whilst the other half reads the script. If two short plays are to be presented, there could be two groups, each of which could manipulate the puppets in one play and read the script for the other play.

One group of children in a class of seven to eight year-olds that I taught worked out a play thus:

1   One child told the others the beginning of a story she had heard

2   The group then discussed how they thought each of the characters would react, and the outcome of these actions. They made a note of each point
3   They acted the play impromptu, scene by scene, with a short discussion of each scene as they came to it. This was taped and the recording used for the show

A play may be written by one child alone or it might be taken from a book and the story adapted for puppets; these are only two of the many possibilities, but whatever method is used the more the children can do for themselves the better.

The puppet play might be tackled as a project for the whole class, or there could be as many as five small groups each producing a short play. The children might consider using different types of puppets: one group could use shadow puppets, another rod puppets, and so on. They should be given guidance in their choice according to the requirements of the play, the capabilities of the children, and the time available.

The children can take a story from history and elaborate upon it; one class I taught took great delight in making up stories about characters in history such as Guy Fawkes, Sir Walter Raleigh, Sir Francis Drake, Queen Elizabeth I, and Mary Queen of Scots. With such plays, the children have to refer to history for the facts, and carry out research for details needed for the play.

In a puppet play, each child can contribute in some way, for a puppet production calls for painters, modellers, scriptwriters, speakers, manipulators, 'electricians' (to look after the lights and tape recorder), and stage-hands. Few subjects can offer such a wide scope for diverse interests to come together and give their individual efforts for a common goal.

Anybody who doubts the value and delights of puppet-making would do well to refer to *An Experiment in Education* by Sybil Marshall; in this book Mrs Marshall gives a charming account of puppetry in her own school before she became a lecturer in education.

WRITING THE SCRIPT

The following are the points that might be considered in group or class discussions before the actual words of the script are obtained. This is one approach to script writing which might be found useful for the upper classes of the junior school. Even children in the juniors are capable of making some sort of critical approach to work of this kind.

It pays to set about the work systematically, beginning with a rough outline of the action. The writer should now see where the climax of the play is to come, and his next task is to list all the points that the audience must know if the climax is to be effective. These points must then be fitted into the story. All too frequently we are presented plays in which the last few minutes are used to explain how a particular situation has been reached. This is clumsy, to say the least, and the audience will not have been able to share fully in that moment of high interest if there are still important facts unexplained at that point. If the important facts are disclosed logically and carefully, then the audience will be kept in suspense and the climax will be meaningful to them; they will become involved in the play. This cannot be over-emphasised. Some readers will no doubt be sceptical about whether juniors can cope with this, but my own class of nine-year-olds have just been working on this and have grasped the idea quite easily. Juniors can understand this provided that a clear explanation is given with illustrations of good and bad plots and endings. Familiar television programmes provide ample material to illustrate the point.

The teacher can also help the children to understand the need to end each scene with something interesting or exciting. They will have to give some thought to leaving the audience with a form of question that has not been answered so that interest is carried forward into the next scene.

Television breaks for advertisements, and serials illustrate this point well.

It is also necessary to consider the audience for whom the play is designed. Is the script really suitable? If the play is being presented by children for their peers, there should be no problem, but if it is being presented by one age group for a much younger audience, this will have to be taken into account. It is surprising how often this is not done.

Puppets need action; they need to move. Still, lifeless puppets that rarely move anything except their mouths are not interesting to watch. The audience might as well listen to the play on a radio or tape recorder as watch such a puppet play, so it is wise to keep speeches and scenes from becoming too long or this tendency will soon creep in.

The first puppet production I ever tackled with children in school taught me a very important lesson which the script writers should consider. It is advisable to limit the number of puppets on stage at any one time, as a large number of puppets requires a large number of manipulators. This causes crowding and struggling for room, and, if you are not careful, soon the manipulation of puppets will be of secondary importance to the fight for space, or, at the very least, some children will be unable to see what they are doing with their puppet.

Finally, if the puppets are made before the final script is written, it helps if the writers have a knowledge of what each puppet does well, and what each does badly. Different puppets do some things better than others, and the script writers can avoid giving to a puppet those actions which the puppet does poorly; for example, if a puppet does not walk very well, it can be arranged for this puppet to have a minimum of walking to do.

Having considered these points, or whichever of them the teacher decides to deal with, the preliminary stages are complete and the children can proceed to obtain their actual script as outlined earlier.

Part Two
THE PUPPET
AND THE PUPPET THEATRE

GLOVE PUPPETS

Glove puppets are usually a little quicker to make than marionettes, and they are able to pick up things easily. They are not restricted by leg movements and can move at high speed, so the puppeteer can keep plenty of action in his plays. Although they are not restricted by leg movements, they are restricted by the operator's hand; because of the shape of the hand, and the shape of a young child's, the glove puppet cannot make the same gestures as a marionette and, in my opinion, rarely has the grace of the marionette unless handled by a very proficient puppeteer.

The glove puppet, because of the hand, cannot leave the ground and its size may be restricted by the size of the hand and what it can cope with. The glove puppet is also restricted in the realms of symbolic puppetry for the shape is partly dictated by the fact that it has to contain a hand, so the number of objects and shapes that can be made is considerably reduced.

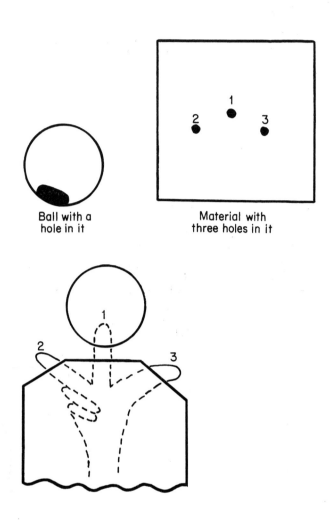

Ball with a
hole in it

Material with
three holes in it

4   THE SIMPLEST GLOVE PUPPET

THE SIMPLEST GLOVE PUPPET

Materials   An old ball; a square or circle of material.

1   Make a hole in the ball. It should just take one finger
2   Cut the material to size and then cut three holes in the material as shown
3   The face is painted on the ball. Wool is glued on for hair
4   Fit the body over the thumb and first two fingers, and then the head over the index finger

The puppet is now ready for use.

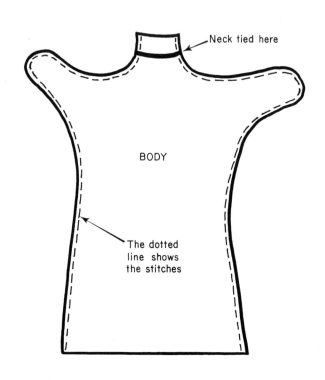

Neck tied here

BODY

The dotted line shows the stitches

Mitten–type hand

Shaped hand

5   THE 'GLOVE' FOR A GLOVE PUPPET

THE 'GLOVE' FOR A GLOVE PUPPET

Materials   Cloth, needle and cotton.

1   Cut out the body shape as shown. You need two pieces
like this
2   Stitch around the edges, as shown by the dotted lines,
leaving unstitched the openings for the neck and the
operator's hand. The 'right' sides of the cloth are stitched
together (inside-out)
3   Hands may be made in the same way and stitched to the
arms separately if desired. They may be the mitten-type or
the shaped hand
4   If hands are made and stitched onto the body, rather
than being part of the mitten, when this has been done, the
'glove' is turned in the right way to hide the seams
5   The glove is then glued and tied to the neck of the
puppet's head, and the puppet is ready for use

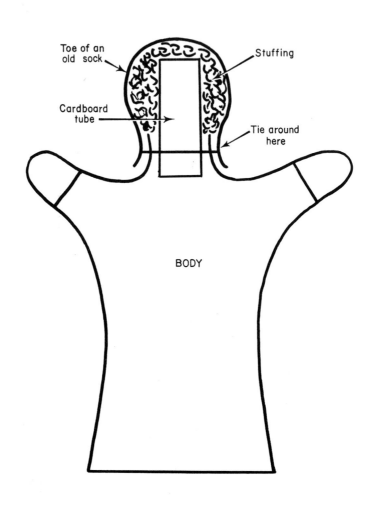

Toe of an
old sock

Stuffing

Cardboard
tube

Tie around
here

BODY

6 THE 'SOCK' PUPPET HEAD

THE 'SOCK' PUPPET HEAD

Materials   An old sock; scraps of material; the body
described above; a piece of soft cardboard.

1   Stuff the toe of the sock with material
2   Cut off the toe of the sock
3   Glue the card into a cylinder, just large enough to hold
the index finger
4   Fit this cardboard insert into the sock
5   Tie the costume neck around the insert and sew the
sock-head to the body
6   The features may be sewn on, as one would embroider
a design, or they may be cut out of coloured felt and glued
or stitched onto the head

*7   Claire manipulates her puppet for the first time whilst another puppet
nears completion*

8   'Sock' puppets, operated by six-year-olds, engage in conversation

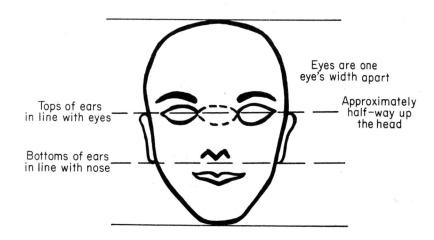

Eyes are one
eye's width apart

Approximately
half-way up
the head

Tops of ears
in line with eyes

Bottoms of ears
in line with nose

9   PROPORTIONS FOR THE HEAD

32

A PAPIER MÂCHÉ HEAD

This type of head may be used for glove or rod puppets or marionettes. A simple adaption to the shape is all that is required for animal heads. The construction is the same.

Materials   Thin cardboard (4″ × 4″); newspaper; glue; papier mâché.

1   Roll the card around the forefinger into a tube and glue it down in position

2   EITHER mix up papier mâché pulp and add this to the tube for a solid papier mâché head

   OR (a) crumple sheets of newspaper around the tube to form a ball shape. This may be held firm by strips of paper glued around the outside of the paper ball

   (b) Build upon this shape with papier mâché. This gives a somewhat lighter head

   If the pulp is built up in small quantities, it will be found much easier to manage and model.

3   The head may be warmed to dry it, but this must be done slowly. When it is dry, the head may be sanded lightly and any cracks filled with more pulp. The head is now ready to paint and use

33

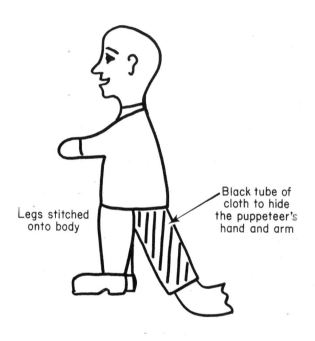

Legs stitched
onto body

Black tube of
cloth to hide
the puppeteer's
hand and arm

10   A GLOVE PUPPET WITH LEGS

GLOVE PUPPETS WITH LEGS

Glove puppets may be given legs. Two tubes of material, stuffed with cloth or foam rubber, and stitched to the inside of the 'glove' are quite adequate for this purpose.

Feet may be cut from a chunk of foam rubber and glued to the ends of the trouser legs. These foam rubber feet may then be covered with felt.

The operating hand is inserted in the puppet behind its legs. Often, with this type of puppet, a black tube of cloth is attached to the inside of the puppet. The arm is inserted through this, and is thus hidden, or at least not so noticeable.

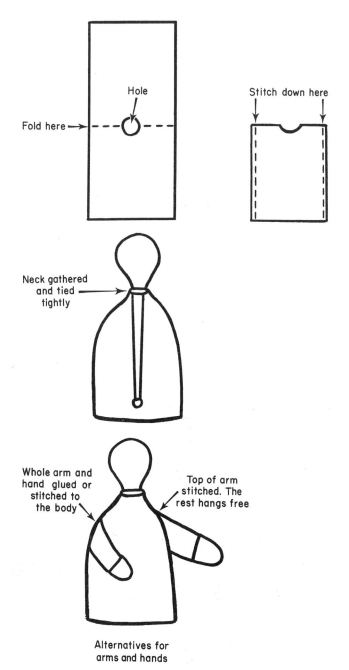

Hole

Fold here →

Stitch down here

Neck gathered
and tied
tightly

Whole arm and
hand glued or
stitched to
the body

Top of arm
stitched. The
rest hangs free

Alternatives for
arms and hands

11 A WOODEN SPOON PUPPET

ROD PUPPETS

Rod puppets, sometimes called stick-puppets, are
extremely easy for children to make and manipulate,
especially the simple forms of rod puppets. They also lend
themselves well to symbolic puppetry.

WOODEN SPOON (ROD) PUPPETS

Materials   An old wooden spoon; material for the costume.

1   Cut a hole for the neck in the middle of a rectangle of
material
2   Fold the material along the centre (inside-out) and stitch
down the sides. Turn the material in the right way to hide
the seams
3   Poke the handle of the spoon down through the hole,
with the hollow in the spoon facing the back of the puppet
4   Gather the costume around the neck and tie it tightly
5   The face is painted on the spoon, and hair may be glued
onto the back of it
6   If sleeves and hands are required, these may be made
from cloth and stitched or glued onto the body

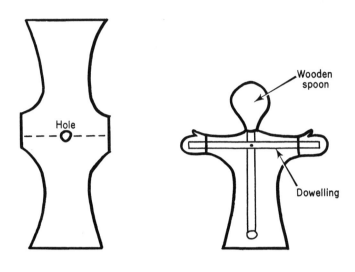

Hole

Wooden spoon

Dowelling

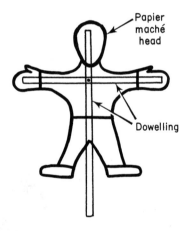

Papier
maché
head

Dowelling

12 ANOTHER ROD PUPPET

ANOTHER ROD PUPPET

This is a variation of the wooden spoon puppet. The arms are formed by having a cross-piece of dowelling nailed, screwed, or tied onto the spoon, as the female figure shows. The costume is put together in similar fashion to the one for the previous rod puppet:

1   The double shape for the costume is cut out. It is folded across the shoulders and the wooden spoon is put in position through the neck-hole
2   The cross-piece is now fastened to the spoon
3   The costume is stitched or glued together as shown by the dotted lines
4   Hands are made as for the glove puppet. These are either stitched or glued onto the ends of the arms

If the puppet is to be male, the shirt is made in the same way as the dress. Trouser legs are made from two tubes of material which are stuffed, and they have foam-rubber feet as for the glove puppet with legs.

Alternatively, as illustrated by the male puppet, the spoon may be replaced by another piece of dowelling. Upon this is mounted a head made from papier mâché or a sock-puppet head.

13   *Children can experiment with their own ideas, as with the head of this rod puppet, being made by nine-year-olds*

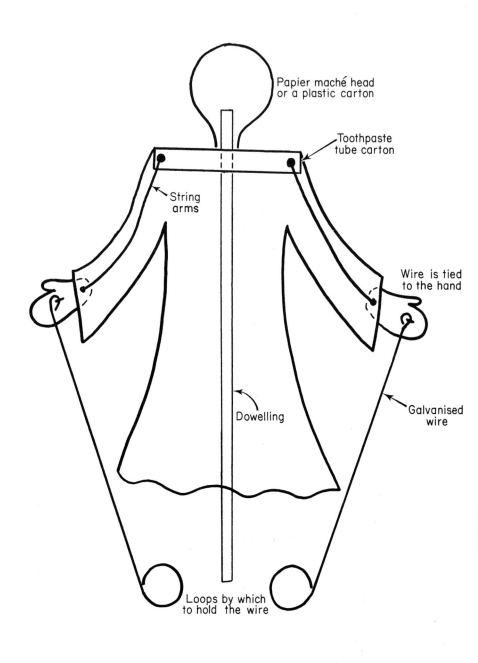

Papier maché head
or a plastic carton

Toothpaste
tube carton

String
arms

Wire is tied
to the hand

Dowelling

Galvanised
wire

Loops by which
to hold the wire

14 A MORE COMPLEX ROD PUPPET

A MORE COMPLEX ROD PUPPET

This puppet is a little more complex than the ones previously described, but it is within the capabilities of a primary school child.

Materials   Papier mâché or a plastic carton; toothpaste carton; string; cardboard; a length of dowelling; two pieces of galvanised wire; material for clothes.

1   The head is made of papier mâché. Alternatively, it may be made from a yogurt or cream carton
2   The dowelling, by which the puppet is supported, is glued into the head. It is pushed through a hole made in the cardboard toothpaste carton, and this is glued in place for the shoulders
3   Pieces of string form the arms, and these are tied onto the cardboard hands
4   The costume hangs from the shoulders and may be gathered at the waist to give more shape to the body
5   Each piece of galvanised wire must have a small loop at one end, and a larger loop at the other end. The small loop is tied onto the hand by string, forming a hand control

The puppet is held up by one hand which holds the dowel. In his free hand, the puppeteer holds the two larger loops of the hand-wires; with these he can operate the hands and arms.

With this type of puppet, the male figure usually has the same sort of long flowing robe as the female puppet.

NOTE   *Galvanised wire is recommended for the hand wires as it is extremely cheap and easily obtained from ironmongers.*

THE SHADOW PUPPET

This is a flat figure which is held between a source of light and an opaque screen. The shadow of the puppet is thrown onto the screen, and the audience watches the shadows from the other side of the screen.

It is an easily made and simply operated puppet, very suitable for children in the primary school.

Materials   Cardboard; coloured cellophane paper; galvanised wire; string, or rivet-type paper fasteners.

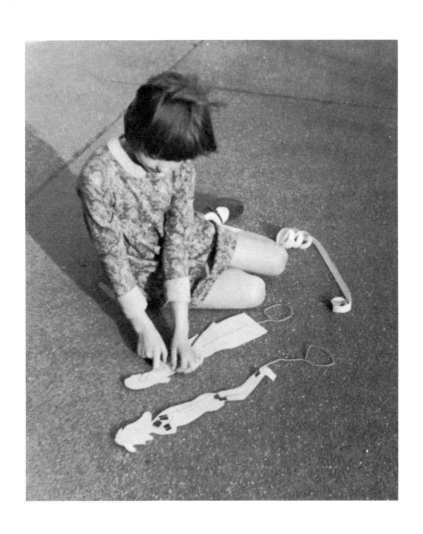

15   Shadow shapes, produced simply and quickly, look intricate and fascinating in silhouette

43

NON-ARTICULATED SHADOW PUPPETS

1   Draw the outline of the figure on fairly stiff cardboard. This will usually need to be a side view so that the puppet can walk across the screen and face other puppets to converse with them
2   Cut out the figure
3   Take a length of wire; make a loop at one end of it and tape it onto the puppet as illustrated

The puppet is held by the wire, the puppeteer being below the level of the screen.

16   *Shadow puppets are so simple to operate as nine-year-old Martin shows*

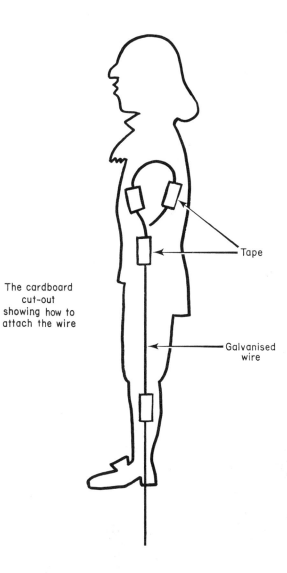

The cardboard
cut-out
showing how to
attach the wire

Tape

Galvanised
wire

ARTICULATED SHADOW PUPPETS

1 and 2 as for non-articulated puppets

3 Cut out separate arms and legs. The arms may be jointed at the elbows and wrists if required; the legs may be jointed at the knees

4 The separate sections are fastened together by making a small hole in each section, threading a piece of string through the holes, and knotting it on either side of the puppet. Instead of string, the parts may be joined with a rivet-type paper fastener

5 The legs can be left to swing free whilst the hand is controlled by a second wire held in the free hand. There is a loop in one end of the wire; a string through the hand is tied to this loop

18 An articulated shadow puppet is laid out ready to be assembled

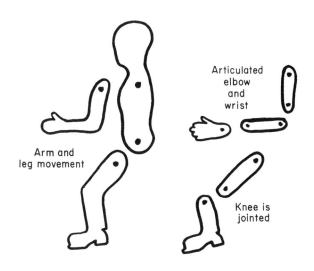

Articulated
elbow
and
wrist

Arm and
leg movement

Knee is
jointed

METHOD OF
FASTENING JOINTS

OR

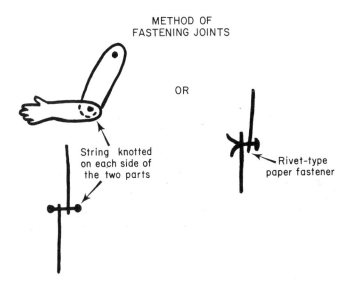

String knotted
on each side of
the two parts

Rivet-type
paper fastener

19 ARTICULATED SHADOW PUPPETS

PATTERNS AND COLOUR
WITH SHADOW PUPPETS

1   Holes may be punched in the cardboard, or pieces cut out for different features, or a pattern made to decorate the costume

2   If colour is required in these spaces, pieces of cellophane paper may be glued over the hole, and the colours will show on the screen

20   Concentration on shadow puppet making: Robert is making a 'human' puppet whilst Colin finishes two animal shapes

SCENERY

I have found shadow puppets to come across well even with no scenery at all. However, if scenery is required on the shadow-screen, cardboard cut-outs, pinned to battens, may be suspended against the screen.

A SIMPLE PUPPET BOOTH
FOR GLOVE AND ROD PUPPETS

A make-shift theatre for glove and rod puppets is easily erected by turning a table on end and acting the puppets over the upper end.

An alternative is to drape a sheet, a tablecloth, or old curtains over a clothes-horse.

A SHADOW PUPPET SCREEN

An excellent screen may be made from an old sheet. Old curtains may be stitched or pinned to the bottom of the screen to hide the operators.

This theatre front may be suspended between two sticks or poles which are held upright by tying them to chairs or tables. A source of light (a window will do in daytime) is required behind the screen to produce the shadow when the puppeteer holds up his cut-out figure from below the level of the screen.

Alternatively, the curtains may be suspended from classroom fixtures such as metal beams across the ceiling. Strings to support the curtains can be tied to safety-pins in the top corners of the screen.

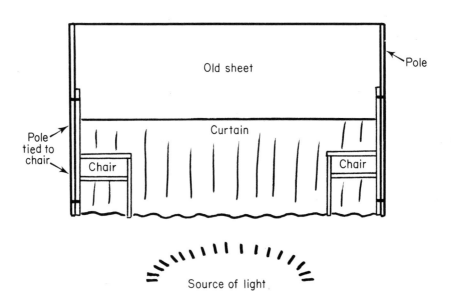

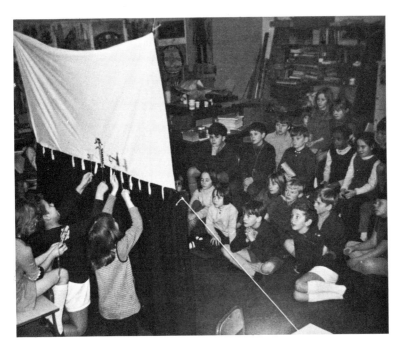

21 *A classroom shadow play, organised in minutes with a screen suspended from the ceiling. Light is supplied through a window*

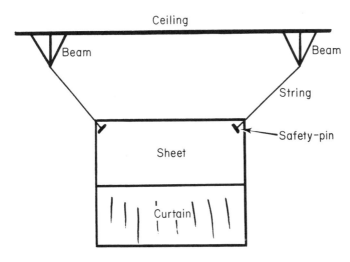

22 A SHADOW PUPPET SCREEN

23 ‘*Thus spake the seraph and forthwith*
Appeared a shining throng...’
The puppets act as a choir sings

THE MARIONETTE

The marionette, or string puppet, has a greater variety of actions than other puppets. It can leave the ground, but cannot pick up objects at random; this, however, can be achieved with extra stringing, magnets, or hooks, but is not usually needed in the primary school anyway. The shape of the puppet can add a lot of character to the marionette, more than is afforded by the shape of the glove puppet.

A criticism often levelled against marionettes is that they are difficult to manipulate, but my experience has shown that even a child of seven to eight years of age can handle a simple marionette quite competently. It may be noted that with an 8-string marionette half of the strings are solely for support, and the other four control the hands and legs; thus, the puppet is not really as complicated as it first appears to the unfamiliar eye.

Marionettes are ideal for 'trick' puppets, and they lend themselves well to symbolic puppetry and to the animation of any object whatever its shape.

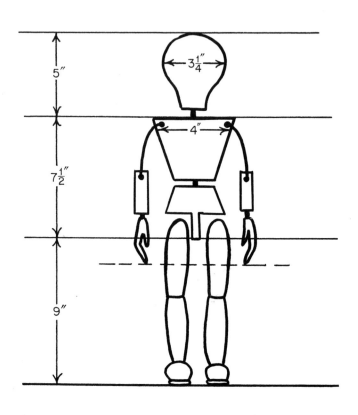

24   AN EXAMPLE OF PROPORTION

PROPORTIONS OF THE MARIONETTE

Some puppeteers advocate the scaling-down to human proportions of the puppet, but the effect is often ludicrous for, surprising though it may seem, a puppet made to human proportions looks out of proportion. Head, hands, and feet should be a little larger than human proportions, and the legs a little short. A puppet made thus is easier to manipulate and is given stronger characterisation.

The hands should be about as long as the distance from the chin to the middle of the forehead, and the feet should be a little longer than the hands. When the arms hang loose, the tips of the fingers should reach to about half-way down the thigh.

Actions and character are influenced a great deal by the puppet's shape and proportions. All too frequently, puppeteers make the common mistake of making all their marionettes far too tall and thin, so losing a lot of character that the body could give.

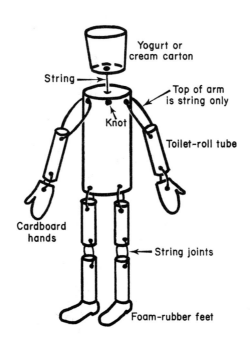

Yogurt or
cream carton

String

Top of arm
is string only

Knot

Toilet-roll tube

Cardboard
hands

String joints

Foam-rubber feet

25 THE TUBE PUPPET

THE TUBE PUPPET

Materials   Yogurt or cream carton; washing-up liquid container; toilet roll tubes; cardboard; string; foam rubber.

1   Make a hole in the bottom of the cream carton and in the bottom of the container for washing-up liquid. Join these by a string which is knotted at each end inside each container. These form the head and body
2   Attach the toilet roll tube arms and legs by loops of string though holes in the tubes. Instead of these tubes, pieces of cardboard may be rolled and glued into the cylindrical shape
3   Cut the hands from cardboard and join them to the arms with string
4   Cut pieces of foam rubber to whatever size and shape desired for the feet and glue (or stitch) them onto the ends of the legs
5   Glue a sheet of paper around the head so that it may be painted
6   Features are painted or glued on (e.g. buttons for eyes, toothpaste tube cap or cork for nose) and then hair (wool) is added

26 *A tube puppet—a marionette—under construction by nine-year-olds*

27 Diana is delighted with this tube puppet
28 The completed tube puppet 'A Roman school master' gives his first lesson

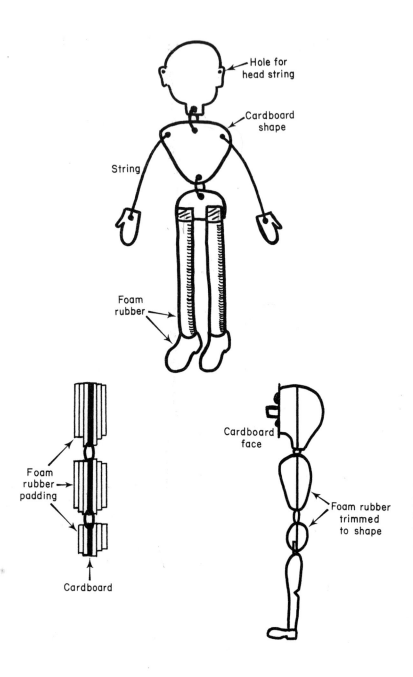

Hole for
head string

Cardboard
shape

String

Foam
rubber

Foam
rubber
padding

Cardboard

Cardboard
face

Foam rubber
trimmed
to shape

29 A PADDED CARDBOARD PUPPET

A PADDED, CARDBOARD PUPPET

Materials   Cardboard, foam rubber, string.

1   The flat shapes of the head and body are cut from strong cardboard. Layers of foam rubber padding are glued to these after the sections of card are tied together
2   The string arms are tied to holes made in the shoulders
3   The hands are cut from strong card and fastened to the cord
4   The legs are made from thick strips of foam rubber which are trimmed to shape with scissors
5   The foam body is also trimmed to shape with scissors
6   The face is made by sticking a cardboard shape over the last layer of padding on the head, adding a nose (e.g. a cork) and eyes (buttons), and then painting the face. Hair is then glued on
7   Foam rubber feet are glued onto the foam legs

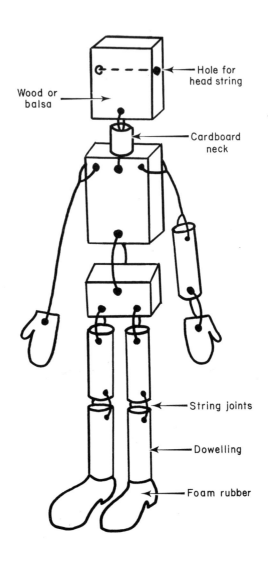

Hole for
head string

Wood or
balsa

Cardboard
neck

String joints

Dowelling

Foam rubber

30 A SIMPLE WOODEN PUPPET

A SIMPLE WOODEN PUPPET

Materials   Balsa wood, or pine, or any soft wood; string; cardboard; $\frac{1}{2}$ in. diameter dowelling.

1   Make a hole in the head and the top of the body. Thread a length of string through these and tie the ends together
2   If the body is in two parts, repeat this with the upper and lower sections
3   The string arms are tied through holes made in the shoulders
4   The hands are cut from strong cardboard and the string arms are tied to them
5   If extra weight in the arms is required, a short piece of dowelling with a hole drilled at each end serves this purpose. It is usually best if this is tied in as the fore-arm
6   A small piece of card may be glued around the neck-string to make a more substantial neck
7   The legs may be made of pieces of $\frac{1}{2}$ in. diameter (or larger) dowelling, joined by string
8   Feet may be cut from foam-rubber and glued to the legs, or wooden blocks, padded and shaped with felt or foam rubber, may be glued and/or screwed to the ends of the legs

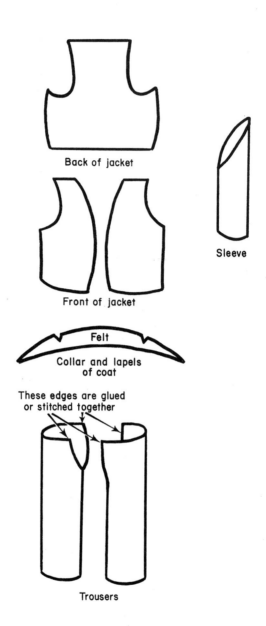

Back of jacket

Front of jacket

Sleeve

Felt

Collar and lapels
of coat

These edges are glued
or stitched together

Trousers

31   DRESSING THE MARIONETTE

DRESSING THE MARIONETTE

The marionette must be dressed before it is strung. Frequently the inexperienced rush into stringing the puppet and then find that they cannot put on the clothes without cutting nearly all the strings.

The clothes may be stitched, but I find the quickest method is to glue the separate parts together with Bostik No. 1 glue. Hems are made by turning up the edge of the cloth and gluing it in place. Some people, however, do not appear to be able to acquire the knack of this method and they would be well advised to keep to sewing the clothes although this takes considerably longer to do.

For trousers, two legs are made by wrapping the cloth around a wide dowel and then gluing one edge on top of the other. These two legs are then glued together at the top. Sleeves are made in the same way as the trouser legs.

A jacket is made in five sections; the sleeves are glued to the coat after the other sections are glued together on the body. Ties and coat lapels are effectively made from coloured pieces of felt. A strip around the neck to form a collar must not be too stiff or too tight or it will restrict the movement of the head.

Soft materials are necessary for puppets' clothes; those materials which are thick and stiff hinder the puppets' actions. In addition, the clothes should not be too tight, especially the sleeves and trouser legs, for this will restrict the joints; there must be maximum freedom at these points.

Finally, if possible, choose the material under artificial lighting if it is to be a large, elaborate production; this will give some idea of what the costume will look like on the stage: it will not look the same as in daylight.

32   The manipulation of a simple 'aeroplane' control is no trouble at all

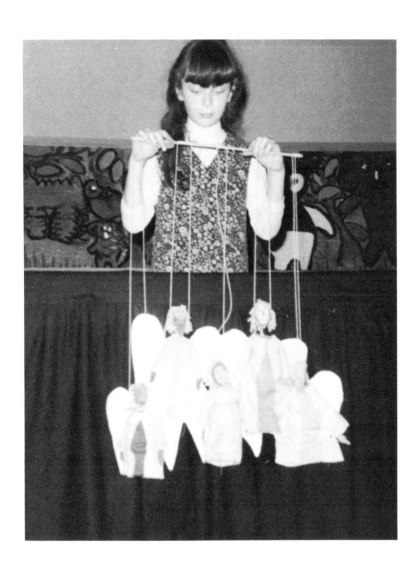

33   For the host of angels, one bar provides sufficient control

A SIMPLE 'AEROPLANE' CONTROL FOR MARIONETTES

This control is made by gluing, screwing, or tying together two pieces of wood in the shape of a cross. A hook for hanging up the puppet may be screwed into the main centre piece.

A string on each side of the cross-piece is tied to each ear in order to support the head (and, in fact, the whole puppet).

A string from each hand is tied to the centre bar.

Leg strings are tied onto a separate cross-bar which is joined to the centre bar by a piece of string. They are attached to the puppet just above the knees. The leg bar may be omitted if it is not required; some younger children might be quite happy to 'walk' the puppet by bouncing it slightly if they cannot cope with leg strings.

The puppet is held in one hand by the centre bar. The free hand operates the hand strings. When it is needed to walk, the leg bar is rocked with a paddling movement.

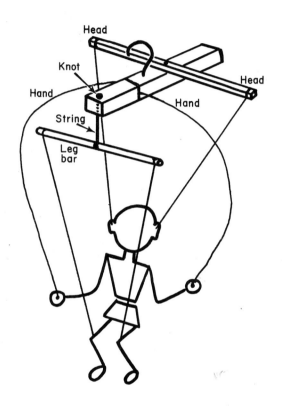

34   A SIMPLE 'AEROPLANE' CONTROL

A MORE COMPLEX 'AEROPLANE' CONTROL

The puppet is walked by 'paddling' the whole control.

If the bars for the head and shoulders were not suspended, but fixed to the control instead, then the head and shoulders would wobble from side to side when the puppet walked. The method for suspending these two bars is exactly the same as for the leg bar on the previous 'aeroplane' control.

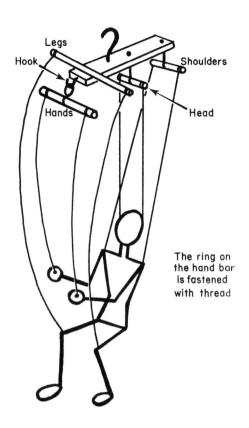

Legs

Hook

Shoulders

Hands

Head

The ring on
the hand bar
is fastened
with thread

A THEATRE FOR ALL TYPES OF PUPPETS

Marionettes may be manipulated over a back-drop (see opposite) with no proscenium-fronted theatre, but I have designed and developed a theatre which can be used for marionettes, shadow, glove, and rod puppets. This can be erected by three children in seven or eight minutes, including fixing the curtains, and it can be dismantled just as quickly.

The frame consists of lengths of $1\frac{1}{2}$ in. × $\frac{3}{4}$ in. pine which bolt together with wing nuts. The foot and angle-strut which support the theatre are screwed together and to the upright which they support. The framework supports two rows of curtains, the top one overlapping the lower one by two or three inches.

When the lower set is opened, a marionette stage is revealed, and if this set is closed and the upper set opened, it becomes a theatre for glove and rod puppets. Fasten a piece of cotton sheet in this opening and it becomes a shadow puppet screen.

This multi-purpose theatre caters for all needs; it packs away neatly and is also cheap to construct. This theatre also allows the working area to be any size, as the curtains can be opened as far or as little as is desired for different occasions.

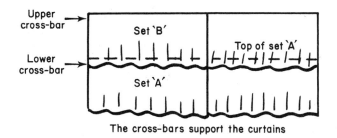

Upper cross-bar →

Lower cross-bar →

Set `B´

Top of set `A´

Set `A´

The cross-bars support the curtains

Pull back set `A´

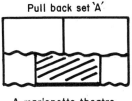

A marionette theatre

Pull back set `B´

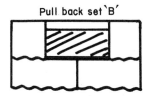

Glove, rod and shadow
puppet theatre
(insert a screen in the
opening for shadow puppets)

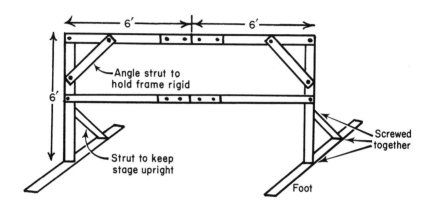

THE FRAME FOR THE THEATRE

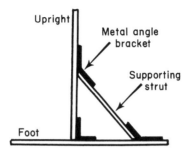

Side view of the upright
and 'foot' of the stage

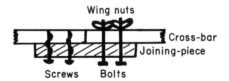

Elevation of the joint
in the cross-bar

THE BACK-CLOTH (OR BACK-DROP)

The back-cloth is the curtain over which the puppeteer manipulates a marionette. In a full proscenium theatre, like the one described on page 72, the back-cloth should be 6 in. higher than the highest point visible to the front row of the audience. When working in the open, in view of the audience, a back-cloth is still used to separate the puppets from the puppeteer, and it will usually be convenient for it to be about waist-height.

A rod, pole, or length of wood, fastened to a chair at each end, will provide a back-drop support. The back-cloth may be pinned to the cross-bar with drawing pins, or it may hang from a curtain wire supported by a few small hooks in the bar.

If the back-cloth is to be plain, suitable colours are black, grey, green, or deep blue. For scenic back-cloths, a good method is to paint with poster colours on unbleached calico, but a very cheap way for children is to paint on long, wide strips of paper which schools often have, or can easily obtain, in large rolls. This paper can be fastened with drawing pins to narrow battens at the top and bottom, and a second scene may be painted on the other side.

37 'We three Kings of Orient are. . .'
The back-drop is a plain black drape supported as described in the text.
The operators stand on a bench

LIGHTING FOR THE
PUPPET THEATRE

Excess of light makes things seem hard; too much darkness
does not admit our seeing them. The mean is excellent.

LEONARDO DA VINCI

The puppet stage must be adequately illuminated. Seeing
the puppets clearly is of outstanding importance. Visibility
should never be discarded for any particular effects.

Strictly speaking, the light from the different sources
should be unequal, either through having the light stronger
from one side, or by having an extra, stronger light overhead.
However, for junior school purposes, I have found two lights
adequate. I prefer two 100 watt reflector spotlights; these
may be held by ordinary lightbulb sockets, but by far the
easiest way of fixing the lights is with photographic
reflectors. Simple reflectors can be purchased quite cheaply
and can be clamped onto the stage in seconds. With these
it is also far easier to adjust the lights to any position.
These reflector spotlights do not burn out; they are not
photographic lights, but are like those used in shop windows.

Ordinary light bulbs may be used in home-made
lamp-holders made from tins, or in light sockets which are
fastened to battens. I feel that the second of these two methods
is suitable for juniors, but not the first although it is
frequently described in books of instruction on puppetry.
My own experience has shown that cutting tins and
fastening light fixtures in them is beyond juniors, apart
from being very dangerous; it therefore becomes an
activity for the teacher rather than for the children. The
type of light socket illustrated is easily attached to a batten,
and may be used for ordinary lights or floodlights of a
similar type to the reflector spotlights mentioned above.
(If the holders are attached to a batten, and not adjustable,
floodlights are preferable to spotlights as they will give a
better spread of light. Spotlights give a better concentration
of light and are excellent if they can be put into the position
required.)

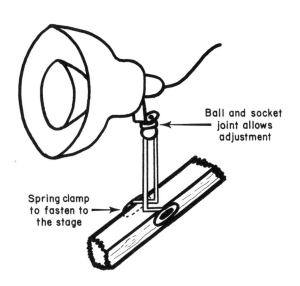

Ball and socket
joint allows
adjustment

Spring clamp
to fasten to
the stage

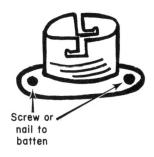

Screw or
nail to
batten

Coloured lighting should be approached with caution, for if it is carelessly used it can obscure visibility. All lights should be placed or shielded in such a way that they do not call undue attention to themselves; inadequately shielded lights produce a dazzling, irritating, and distracting effect upon the audience.

Coloured lighting does, however, provide many opportunites for expression of mood and feeling. It can add so much to the tone and the effectiveness of a play that it is well worth experimenting with coloured lights; this is, of course, really a whole field of art in itself. Coloured light bulbs can be purchased quite cheaply. Alternatively (and I prefer this method) coloured filters of Cinemoid may be used on the ordinary lights. If any difficulty is found in buying small quantities of this material, often theatres, theatrical companies, ballrooms, etc have off-cuts from the large rolls of Cinemoid that they purchase, and they are frequently willing to give the small pieces for use in primary schools.

This work can lead the children into studying the symbolism of colours, how different moods can be conveyed, how to represent bright sunlight, a dark night, or moonlight, and even how filters work by absorbing some of the component colours in a ray of light. Motivated sufficiently by this exciting art form, the children want to look into, and to understand, ideas as diverse as these; this is just an example of how, through puppetry, so many teaching points can arise and how so many can be integrated, for, when wisely used, puppetry can be a really dynamic art form.